arTrageous!

Jennifer McCully

This library edition published in 2016 by Walter Foster Jr.,
an imprint of Quarto Publishing Group USA Inc.
6 Orchard Road, Suite 100
Lake Forest, CA 92630

Distributed in the United States and Canada by
Lerner Publisher Services
241 First Avenue North
Minneapolis, MN 55401 U.S.A.
www.lernerbooks.com

First Library Edition

Library of Congress Cataloging-in-Publication Data

Names: McCully, Jennifer, author.
Title: ARTrageous! / By Jennifer McCully.
Description: Lake Forest : Quarto Publishing Group USA Inc., 2016. |
   "Featuring 25 drawing, painting & mixed media projects to create and
   inspire."
Identifiers: LCCN 2016000205 | ISBN 9781942875109 (hardcover)
Subjects: LCSH: Mixed media (Art)--Technique--Juvenile literature.
Classification: LCC TT157 .M4453 2016 | DDC 745.5--dc23
LC record available at http://lccn.loc.gov/2016000205

Printed in USA
9 8 7 6 5 4 3 2 1

Contents

Introduction * *

Imagination, discovery, exploration, taking risks, and having fun are what this book is all about! Along the way, you'll discover colorful accidents and mistakes that will make you go "ooh" and "ahh" in almost every project, helping you create one-of-a-kind pieces of art!

The projects in this book are considered mixed media art—an art style that has no rules! There is no right way or wrong way to do things, no limits, and no experience needed. You are free to create as you wish! Each project offers basic steps and techniques to guide your creative spirit on a journey that will end with a unique creation to share with family and friends. Feel free to use my instructions as examples, and make the art your own.

Being fearless is a must! Be brave, and try every technique you see. If you don't like the results, try it your own way. Creating from the heart allows your soul to create with passion and purpose. New colors and textures—and smiles—will evolve as you discover the artist within. As you complete each project, your desire to create will grow as your creative spirit starts to truly take flight. Artful ideas will continue to emerge, and a newfound happiness for color, texture, and beautiful things will inspire you daily.

I encourage you to share your projects with me. I am constantly amazed by all of the creativity and color in our wonderful world that has yet to be discovered! To share your projects, please visit www.jennifermccully.com for my contact information. I can't wait to see what you come up with!

Live artfully,

Jennifer McCully

Jennifer is also the author of There are No Mistakes in Art—a little book that takes artists of all ages on a colorful journey about art, courage, and endless possibilities! Visit www.jennifermccully.com to learn more.

Dedication

For Casa McCully—my creative nest, the place that I love to be the most—around my favorite people in the whole wide world. Just like mixed media art, each of you brings vibrant colors, texture, and joyful chaos to my life. Your flicks and drips make their way into my art in so many different forms, and I could not be more grateful.

And for Phil, my wonderful husband, whom I simply cannot breathe without. Thank you for your endless love and support, and the never-ending happy moments you give me each day. Our crazy little love story inspires my creative spirit in so many ways.

Tools & Materials

One of the best things about mixed media art is that you can use almost anything! Each project in this book tells you what you'll need to complete it, so be sure to check the supplies list before you begin. You should be able to find all of these materials at your local art & craft store. Here are some of the basic tools and materials to help you get started.

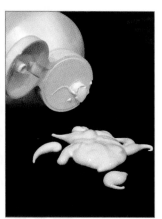

Gesso Gesso is an important tool for preparing—or *priming*—canvas or wood for painting. Similar to white paint, gesso is thinner in consistency and dries hard, making the surface stiff. Gesso makes the surface slightly textured and ready to accept paint. It also helps create a nice base for applying new colors on top of other colors.

Drawing Pencil, Eraser & Sharpener Keep a sharpened pencil nearby for sketching on your paper or canvas. Make a mistake? That's okay—that's what erasers are for!

Mod Podge® Mod Podge is an all-in-one glue and sealant that can be used on any surface. I always use Mod Podge for creating mixed media artwork. Mod Podge goes on white, but dries clear! Use a coat both underneath and on top of layers to secure them.

Watercolor Crayons & Pencils Watercolor crayons (or water-soluble wax pastels) and pencils are fun to draw with. I like to use them to outline parts of my art. You can also go over marks made with these tools with a wet brush, turning the color into a watercolor wash! Pictured here are watercolor crayons; watercolor pencils look just like colored pencils.

Oil Pastels Oil pastels are smooth, creamy sticks that can be used to accent or complement artwork. Like watercolor crayons, I like to use oil pastel to outline elements of my artwork, such as words or the edges of a canvas.

Markers & Pens Add color to your artwork with your favorite markers, felt-tipped pens, and permanent markers. Make sure you have some fine-tipped markers or pens for outlining or writing words.

Acrylic Paints Acrylic paint is nontoxic and water-based, which means you can use water to thin it and clean your paintbrushes and any other tools. This kind of paint dries quickly and can be mixed with fun mediums, gels, and pastes for cool effects!

Watercolor Paints Just use a little bit of water to turn cakes or pans of watercolors into pretty, fluid paint! You can also find watercolor paint in tubes.

Paintbrushes & Palette Knife

You'll need brushes of all sizes for creating mixed media artwork. Big flat brushes are good for painting backgrounds. Small round brushes are good for painting details. A palette knife is a fun tool to paint thickly with acrylic. You can also use it to scrape and "draw" designs in wet paint!

Surfaces You can create awesome mixed media art on lots of different surfaces. The most common are canvas, watercolor paper, fabric, wood, and cardboard.

Scrapbook or Specialty Handmade Paper Fun decorative papers add a splash of color, texture, and pattern to mixed media artwork. Collect papers that catch your eye and put them to artistic use! You can also use tissue paper, wrapping paper, and newspaper.

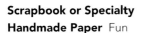

Hole Punches Hole punches come in various sizes. You should have a regular hole punch and a very small hole punch. An eyelet punch (pictured) or grommet punch is also helpful for making holes in cardboard, fabric, or canvas.

Scissors & Craft Knife Scissors are great for cutting papers, felt, and ribbons. For cutting heavier items like cardboard, a craft knife works better. A craft knife blade is very sharp. Be very careful, and always work with an adult when using this tool.

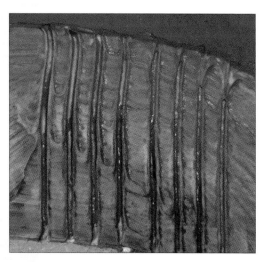

Molding Paste Add a bit of molding paste to paint to create a thick mixture that can be "sculpted" with brushes or a palette knife. You can also use it underneath paint to create a textured base.

Glass Bead Gel This medium contains small glass beads in a thick gel. The beads create a textured surface as they reflect light. Smooth the gel over light paint colors with a palette knife.

Paper Plate Palette Use a paper plate to hold and mix your acrylic paints. Put just a little bit of each color on the plate. You can always add more!

PROTECTING YOUR ARTWORK

It's always a good idea to protect your artwork, especially if you use materials that can smudge, such as oil pastel or watercolor crayons. I recommend that you always spray finished artwork with a matte spray varnish, but it is optional. Work with spray varnish in a well-ventilated area—preferably outside. Always use varnish with an adult. Matte spray varnish is not listed in the supplies lists for the projects in this book, but a spray can icon is included with each project that I recommend varnishing.

Additional Materials

- Fabric
- Ribbons, yarn & twine
- Washi tape
- Stamps & stencils
- Magazine cuttings
- Plastic squeeze tube with pointed tips
- Brads
- Heavy-duty needle & thread
- Jewelry pliers & wire
- Hot glue gun
- Industrial-strength glue

Art Techniques * *

There are many techniques you can use in mixed media art. On the next few pages I'll show you some of the techniques used to create the projects in this book. But don't be afraid to experiment and explore other techniques!

Mark-making

You can make all kinds of marks with pencils, markers, paintbrushes, and more!

Markers and pens come in different sizes and tip widths. Experiment with mark-making utensils to see what kinds of marks you can make.

You can use *crosshatching* to develop depth and interest. Crosshatching is simply making sets of lines that cross each other, like in this owl.

Similar to crosshatching, you can use *stippling* to suggest depth and add movement. To stipple, just use small dots. Placing many dots close together creates a darker tone. Making fewer dots further apart creates a lighter tone.

Dripping & Splattering

To add drips to your work, load a flat paintbrush with watered-down acrylic paint and press the tip into the top of the canvas. Hold the canvas upright to encourage the paint to drip down. The paint needs to be diluted enough to drip all the way down the canvas, so add more water if you need to.

To splatter, alternate dipping your brush in paint and water (a few times each) to make the paint thin enough to splatter freely off the brush. Then hold the brush over your art surface and tap it with a finger near the tip.

Other Acrylic Painting Techniques ✳ ✳

Use a sponge to dab paint onto your artwork.

Use a palette knife to "draw" in wet paint by using the pointed tip to scrape away paint.

To create a hint of color or pattern, let acrylic paint sit on the surface for a few seconds, and then wipe it away with a paper towel. I like to use this technique to add subtle patterns.

Watercolor Paint & Crayons

You can change the darkness of watercolor paint by simply adding water!

Smudge or smear watercolor crayons with a cotton swab. You can also use a damp cotton swab to activate the pigment on paper and create a watercolor wash.

Oil Pastels

You can smear, smudge, and blend oil pastel markings with a cotton swab or your finger.

Mini Book * * of Art

SUPPLIES

- 4 cardboard squares (8" x 8")
- Paintbrushes
- Gesso
- Mod Podge®
- Scrapbook paper or handmade paper
- Scissors
- Acrylic paint (various colors)
- Black watercolor crayon
- Pencil and sharpener
- Stencil patterns (various)
- Hole punch
- 3 book rings (1")
- Fabric strips (optional)

STEP 1 Cut out four 8" x 8" squares of cardboard, preferably from a shipping box.

STEP 2 Cover each square, front and back, with gesso. I suggest working on a vinyl tablecloth or a large piece of wax paper to prevent the art from sticking to the work area. Allow the gesso to dry completely.

ARTIST TIP

- Create the pages for this book in any order you choose. You can also add more pages if you like!
- When painting the squares with acrylic paint, allow the first side to dry completely before working on the other.
- Keep in mind how your book will be assembled, and paint all of your cardboard squares in the same direction so that they can be turned and read like the pages of a book.
- Varnish each book page, front and back, before assembling with the metal rings. Remember to allow the first side to dry completely before varnishing the other!

Page 1: Decoupage & Bloom

STEP 1 Brush Mod Podge on a cardboard square and lay a collage of paper in place, pressing gently to smooth it out. Once dry, trim excess paper from the sides with scissors. Then add a layer of Mod Podge on top of the paper.

STEP 2 Once the background is completely dry, use acrylic paint to add a flower and stem. You can use any color you like!

STEP 3 Add the word "bloom" (or your word of choice) with a black watercolor crayon.

Page 2: Color Outside the Lines

STEP 1 Use acrylic paint to outline rows of circles for the background.

STEP 2 Once the circles are dry, splatter paint in random places on the board.

STEP 3 When the paint splatters are dry, use a paintbrush to write the words or phrase of your choice—fill up the entire background.

Page 3: Unleash Your Creative Spirit

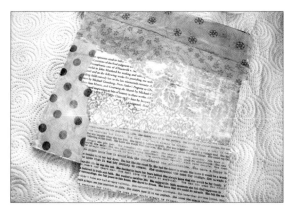

STEP 1 Use Mod Podge to glue a collage of paper over the entire background of a square. Once dry, trim excess paper from the sides and brush Mod Podge over the paper. Allow the paper to dry completely.

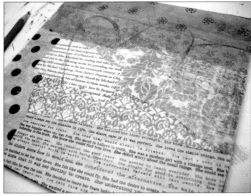

STEP 2 Use a pencil to sketch a heart and wings on the collage.

STEP 3 Paint the heart with watered-down acrylic paint so that the detail in the background peeks through. If there is too much paint, simply dampen a paper towel and rub or blot some of the paint from the cardboard. Then use gesso to paint the wings with a small brush. If you like, add some paint splatters!

STEP 4 Print words or phrases from a standard printer, cut them out, and glue them to the cardboard with Mod Podge. Once dry, outline the hearts, wings, and phrases with a black watercolor crayon.

Page 4: Find Your Happy Place

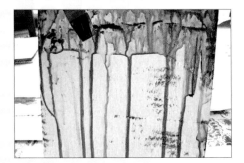

STEP 1 Spread watered-down acrylic paint across the top of the background with a large brush, allowing it to drip down in heavy lines. Let dry.

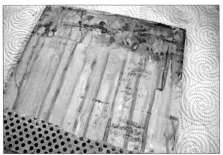

STEP 2 Paint over the background with a light, diluted paint color. Then use Mod Podge to glue a strip of paper along the bottom to act as "grass"—it doesn't have to be green!

STEP 3 Draw a tree outline with a pencil. Then paint the tree with acrylic paint—try to stay inside the lines!

STEP 4 Cut out leaf shapes from a magazine or scrapbook paper. Glue the leaves onto the tree with Mod Podge. Then add another layer of Mod Podge over the leaves to secure them.

STEP 5 Print words or a phrase of your choice onto paper, cut them out, and use Mod Podge to glue them to the cardboard. When the paint and Mod Podge are dry, outline the tree, leaves, and words with a black watercolor crayon.

Page 5: Be Kind

STEP 1 Use a stencil to paint a background on the page.

STEP 2 When the background is dry, add some paint splatters. Cut a heart shape out of scrapbook paper or specialty handmade paper. Discard the heart cut-out or save it for another project.

STEP 3 Use Mod Podge to glue the paper (with heart shape removed) onto the cardboard. Add strips of paper to the sides of the square to frame the heart outline. Then cut out six shapes from an old dictionary or phone book for the phrase "Be Kind." You can use another phrase if you wish! Add the squares to the cardboard with Mod Podge.

STEP 4 Once the art is dry, use a black watercolor crayon to write the letters of your chosen phrase inside the squares, and then outline each square.

Page 6: Peace. Love. Art.

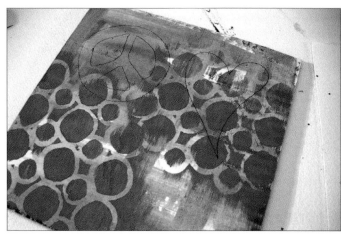

STEP 1 Paint the background a soft color. Once dry, use another color from the same color family to stencil a pattern over the background.

STEP 2 When the pattern is dry, draw a peace sign and a heart.

STEP 3 Cut a heart out of paper and use Mod Podge to glue it in place. Paint the peace sign. Then use a brush to paint the word "art" underneath. Try adding some paint splatters! When everything is dry, roughly outline the peace sign and heart with a black watercolor crayon.

Pages 7 & 8: BE YOUtiful

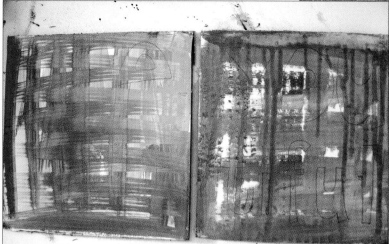

STEP 1 Use two colors in the same color family to create a crisscross pattern on the cardboard square. Let one color dry before adding the second. Paint a similar background on two pieces of cardboard.

STEP 2 When the backgrounds are dry, use a pencil to outline the words or phrase of your choice.

STEP 3 Paint all of the letters with gesso. Try to stay inside the lines! Let dry.

STEP 4 Paint the letters with a variety of acrylic paint colors. Once dry, splatter a little bit of paint on both squares. When all the paint is dry, outline the letters with a black watercolor crayon.

The Finishing Touches

STEP 5 Varnish all of the book pages, punch three holes in each one (make sure you punch the correct sides), and use book rings to bind the pages together. You can tie a couple of strands of fabric around the rings for a little extra flair!

Glass Vase with Cereal-Box Flowers

SUPPLIES

- 1 small glass bottle
- 1 empty cereal box
- Gesso
- Acrylic paints (various colors)
- Mod Podge
- Black watercolor crayon
- Paintbrushes
- Lightweight scrapbook paper or handmade paper
- 2 brads (decorative or non-decorative)
- 1/8-inch hole punch
- Funky yarn (optional)
- Colored twine (optional)
- Heavy-gauge wire
- Jewelry pliers or wire cutters
- Industrial-strength glue (such as E600)
- Dry rice (to hold flowers in vase)

STEP 1 Start with an empty glass bottle, removing the label if it has one.

STEP 2 Use a large brush to apply Mod Podge all over the bottle, wrapping paper around it. Mold the paper onto the bottle with your hands and continue brushing with coats of Mod Podge. You can add several different papers if you choose! Thin paper will stick well.

STEP 3 Once the bottle is completely dry, brush on a light coat of gesso. I put a dab of gesso on my fingers and rubbed it into the dried paper.

STEP 4 Once the gesso is dry, add drips all around the top of the bottle with a paintbrush, acrylic paint, and water.

STEP 5 Add words. You can write them yourself or use printed words. Add twine to the top of the bottle by applying a generous layer of Mod Podge first and then wrapping the twine around it. Finish with more Mod Podge. Once everything is dry, outline the edges of the word strips with a black watercolor crayon and add funky ribbon or yarn to the top of the vase! Add dry rice to the inside of the bottle to hold the flowers!

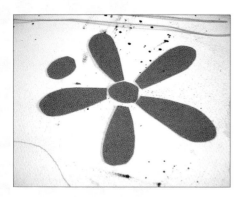

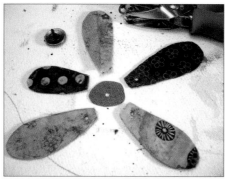

ARTIST TIP
Lay your petals on wax paper or a vinyl tablecloth to dry. Flip them over occasionally so that both sides dry evenly.

STEP 6 Cut 10 petals for two flowers out of an empty cereal box. They don't all need to be the same size or width. Lay them out to see if they go well together. Cut out two circles for the centers of the flowers.

STEP 7 Cover each petal front and back with thin paper using Mod Podge on both sides. Let the petals completely dry, and trim off any excess paper. Use a 1/8-inch hole punch to punch holes near the end of each petal and in the centers of the circles.

STEP 8 Using a brad, build each flower by pushing the brad through the center circle first. Then add five petals behind it, arranging them as you go. When you are happy with the layout of the petals, clamp the brad ends down to hold the "shape" in place.

STEP 9 Add a wire for each flower stem. Using a pair of household pliers or jewelry pliers, make a slight circle at the end of each wire strip. Glue in place with industrial-strength glue. I used a 10" piece of wire for one flower and a 12" piece for the other. Add the flowers to your completed vase.

Mosaic Elephant

SUPPLIES

- 16" x 20" canvas
- Paintbrushes
- Acrylic paint (various colors)
- Pencil and sharpener
- Stencil patterns (various)
- Mod Podge
- Scrapbook paper or handmade paper
- Small plastic squeeze tubes (with multiple tips)
- Palette knife (plastic or stainless steel)
- Oil pastels (various colors)
- Black watercolor crayon
- Fine-point rubber shaper tool (optional)

STEP 1 Make your mark! Start with some splashes of color by tapping a loaded paintbrush near the tip of the brush. Dip the brush in water a few times, alternating between water and paint, to make the paint loose enough to "splatter" off your brush.

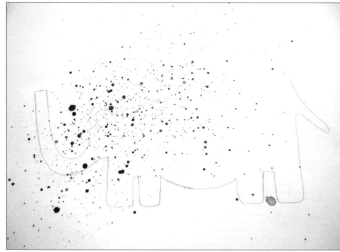

STEP 2 After the paint splatters are completely dry, draw an elephant (or other animal of your choice) with a pencil. Start with a basic shape—just an outline.

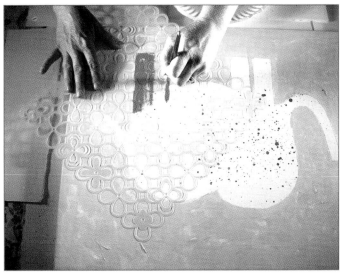

STEP 3 Start painting the background, being careful not to color the elephant. I think it's fun to leave random white spots throughout the canvas. It's okay if your paint is chunky in some areas—chunky spots add more texture!

STEP 4 Use a stencil to add a colored pattern to the elephant. Be careful not to stencil outside the outline, and try not to fill in the whole elephant. I used two different stencils.

STEP 5 Once the stencil design is dry, use Mod Podge to glue various papers in the elephant's body. Don't cover all of the pretty patterns that you just painted! You can rip pieces of paper or cut shapes to fit within the elephant's outline.

ARTIST TIP
Use a larger brush for gluing. When adding paper to the elephant's body, brush glue onto the canvas first. Arrange the paper one section at a time, flatten, and then add more glue right on top. Don't worry—Mod Podge dries clear!

STEP 6 Once dry, add a swoosh of grass across the bottom of the canvas with a thick brush.

STEP 7 Add grass-blades. I like to use a plastic squeeze bottle to add individual blades and squiggly lines. When adding paint to the squeeze bottle, add a very small amount of water as well to thin the paint and make it come out of the tube easier.

STEP 8 Next paint some flowers in different shapes! Half of my flowers are simple circles and the other half are crisscross patterns.

STEP 9 Once the flowers are dry, add stems and leaves with a smaller plastic squeeze tube and tip.

STEP 10 Time to add some detail! Mix two different shades of yellow together to paint the sun. I left some chunky paint in the sun's center. While the yellow paint is still wet, add a touch of orange on the rays.

Adding the Bird

Draw the shape of the bird in pencil.

Once you're happy with the bird's shape, start adding paint.

I used three different shades of green to paint my bird. Use a smaller brush to stay within the lines.

STEP 11 To make the grass look more blended, use a palette knife to randomly add another shade of green.

STEP 12 Use a fine-point rubber shaper tool or the end of a paintbrush to add small details to the flowers and in any white areas on the elephant. Don't forget about the flowers' centers! I like to use oil pastels to quickly sketch in the centers, but you can also use paint.

STEP 13 For the finishing touches, add an eye for the elephant and the bird. Add some feathers to the bird's wing, using paper or paint. Once everything is completely dry, outline the elephant and bird with a black watercolor pencil. Watercolor pencils are erasable, so don't worry if you make a mistake. Don't forget to sign your new masterpiece! To protect your art, varnish the finished piece.

Wire Bird Mobile

SUPPLIES

- Wood shapes/figures (such as a bird or heart)*
- Paintbrushes
- Gesso
- Acrylic paint (various colors)
- Heavy aluminum craft wire (10 or 12 gauge)
- Jewelry wire cutters
- Flat-nose jewelry pliers
- 16 to 20 long fabric strips (approximately 1" x 14")
- 20 to 25 short fabric strips (approximately 1" x 4")
- 2 or 3 wooden clothespins
- Twine (natural)
- Drill (optional)**
- Small metal keyhole (optional)
- Sturdy cardboard (optional)
- Utility or craft knife (optional)**
- Hole punch (optional)

*Look for wood shapes at your local art & craft store or online craft supplier. If possible, use shapes with pre-drilled holes in them. You can also use sturdy cardboard instead of wood.
**Adult supervision required

STEP 1 If not predrilled, drill holes in the wood shapes. I drilled a hole through the top of the heart and a small hole in my wood bird to insert a small keyhole. You can also use sturdy cardboard for the shapes: Simply draw your shapes and cut them out with a utility or craft knife; then use a hole punch to add holes.

STEP 2 Paint the shapes with a coat of gesso. Once dry, paint each piece however you wish! I chose to paint the heart red and splatter white paint across it. I used two shades of blue for the bird and added patterned paper for the wing. Don't forget to give the bird an eye!

STEP 3 Make three circles with the heavy aluminum craft wire. You might want to use round objects as templates, such as mixing bowls or balls. The smaller circle should be approximately 6" in diameter, and the two larger circles should be approximately 7½" in diameter. Use jewelry wire cutters to snip the wire. Then use flat-nose jewelry pliers to create a simple loop on each end of the wire to connect the two ends together.

STEP 4 Start wrapping the long fabric strips around each wire circle. Tie a knot to attach the fabric to the wire where the two ends meet. Then hold the strip very tightly and begin wrapping it around the wire.

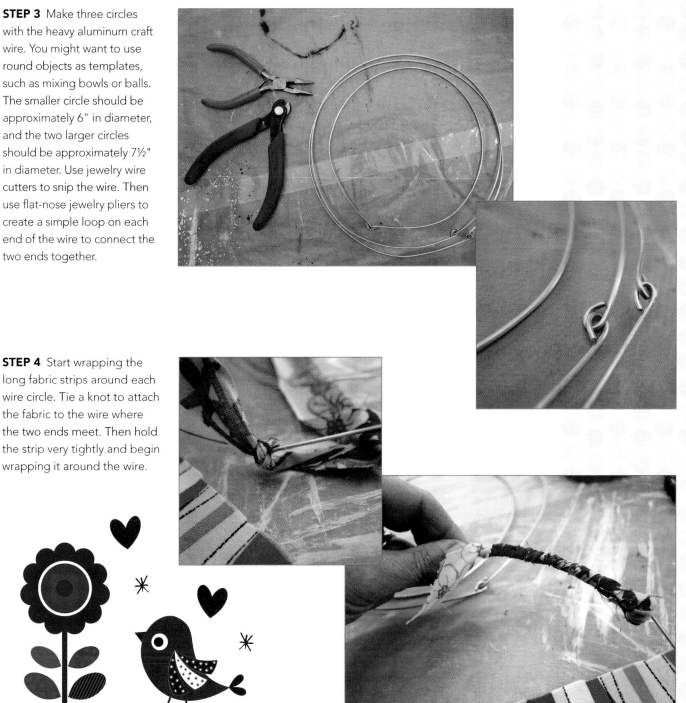

STEP 6 Continue this process until the entire circle is covered in fabric. Use the short strips of fabric to tie knots along the way to keep the long strips tight and connected.

STEP 5 When you reach the end of a strip, take another long strip of fabric and overlap the first, wrapping it around the wire a few times. Use a clothespin to keep the wrapped fabric in place while you tie a knot with a shorter strip of fabric around the overlapped strips to help secure them together. Tuck in the edges of the knotted strip as you begin to wrap the next section of wire.

STEP 7 Repeat this process with the other two circles.

STEP 8 Now it's time to connect all the pieces together! Crisscross the two larger circles by sliding one into the other. Then tie them together with a short strip of fabric on the top and bottom. Attach the smaller circle to the top of the two larger circles. Use additional strips of fabric to attach the bird and heart so that they hang in the circles. Use a piece of twine to create a loop at the top to hang the mobile from a ceiling hook.

Mixed Media Surfboard

SUPPLIES

- Large piece of cardboard
- Pencil and eraser
- Scissors or craft knife*
- Ruler
- Acrylic paint (various colors)
- Paintbrushes
- Rubber tip tool (optional)
- Fine-tipped markers
- Watercolor crayons or oil pastels
- D-ring hanger
- Hot glue gun*

*Adult supervision required

STEP 1 Draw a simple surfboard shape on a piece of cardboard, and cut it out. My surfboard is 9" x 28". You can make yours as big or as small as you like!

ARTIST TIP

This surfboard art can be as simple or as detailed as you wish! I made a simple, vibrant background so that my words would show up well. If you're not adding words, try including cool designs—a tribal pattern, an intricate set of flowers, or polka dots!

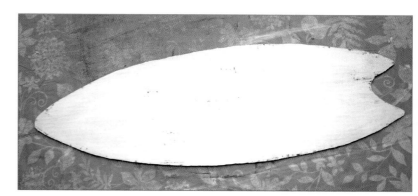

STEP 2 Paint the entire surfboard white. Since cardboard is usually dark brown, painting a base coat of white will help make your background colors nice and vibrant! Let the paint dry completely before adding more color.

STEP 3 Draw a design on the surfboard. I drew a curvy, wave-like line to separate the top and bottom of the board. Use vibrant colors to paint your design with acrylic paint. Then let the paint dry completely.

STEP 4 When the background paint is dry, use fine-tipped markers to doodle in the white part of the surfboard. Any pattern will do—make your art unique!

STEP 5 Next pencil in the words or phrase you want to put on your board. You could even use your name!

STEP 6 Use a small brush to paint in the letters. You might need to use two layers of paint to fully cover the pencil lines. Then add more design elements to the surfboard. Try using a round object, such as a jar lid, to stamp white circles on the board.

STEP 7 Use a rubber tip tool or the handle end of a paintbrush to add small dots around the circles or other design elements. Then roughly outline the words with a watercolor crayon or oil pastel. Add some paint splatters!

STEP 8 Once you are done decorating your surfboard, attach a d-ring hanger to the back with hot glue. You can also simply prop the board up against the wall on a shelf!

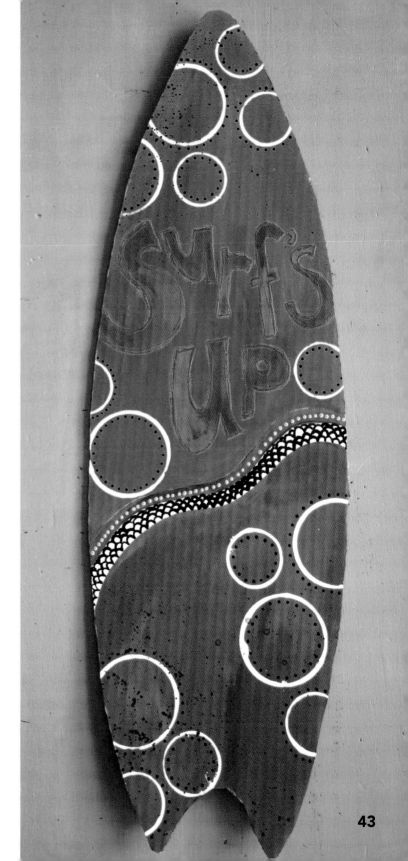

"I am ..." Art on Wood

SUPPLIES

- 12" x 24" piece of birch wood
- Scrapbook or specialty handmade paper
- Scissors
- Mod Podge
- Printed words
- Pencil and eraser
- Black watercolor pencil
- Paintbrush (small)
- Black acrylic paint
- Brown oil pastel
- Sawtooth hanger and hammer*

*Adult supervision required

STEP 1 Glue strips of paper onto the wood. I like to rip the strips for rough edges. Apply the strips with a coat of Mod Podge underneath and on top of the strips. Trim excess paper once dry.

ARTIST TIP

If you use vibrant papers, such as hot pink or turquoise, use white acrylic paint for your words instead of black so that they show up better.

STEP 2 I love to use different font types, so I printed my words in the fonts I want to duplicate. Use a sharpened pencil or a black watercolor pencil to write and draw the words onto your art. Make sure to space the words out so that the art is filled from top to bottom.

STEP 3 Fill in the words with black paint and a very small paintbrush. This is one time that I like to stay in the lines!

STEP 4 Splatter black paint in random areas on the art. It gives the words a magical presence, as if they were splattered into those exact spots! Rub a brown oil pastel along all four edges of the wood. Then smear it onto the art with your fingers, giving the edges a worn look.

STEP 5 If varnishing, let dry before adding a sawtooth hanger on the back!

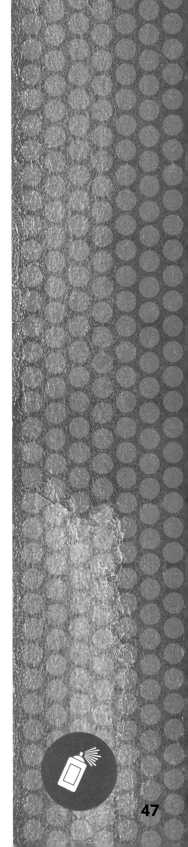

Motivational Mirror

SUPPLIES

- Small, unfinished wood mirror (approx. 10" x 10")
- Painter's tape
- Gesso
- Paintbrushes
- Acrylic paint (various colors)
- Decorative stencil (optional)
- Paper towel
- Printed words
- Pencil and eraser
- Black watercolor pencil

STEP 1 Cover the exposed mirror with painter's tape to protect. Then add two coats of gesso to the wood so you can start with a clean white background for your art.

ARTIST TIP

If you can't find a small, unfinished mirror, you can use a colored wood mirror. Simply paint a coat of gesso over the wood first to cover the color.

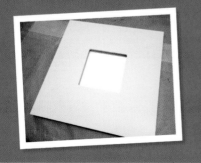

STEP 2 Use a medium-to-large paintbrush to quickly brush on a coat of color—the mirror instantly comes to life with just this one splash of color! There's no need to cover the mirror entirely.

STEP 3 While the paint is slightly damp, use a decorative stencil to add additional color. Allow the stenciled pattern to sit for a couple of seconds, and then wipe it off with a paper towel. This creates texture, leaving faint suggestions of pattern. The two colors mix together to create a washed look.

Using the stencil

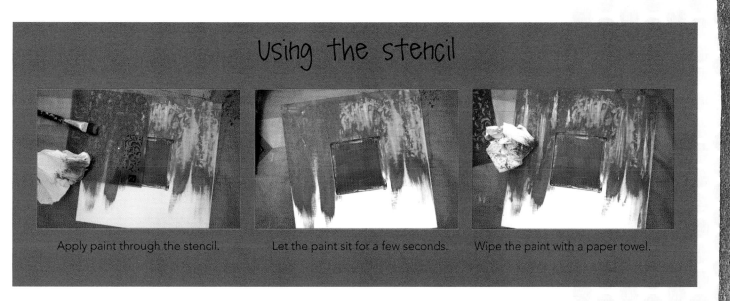

Apply paint through the stencil.   Let the paint sit for a few seconds.   Wipe the paint with a paper towel.

STEP 4 Once the background color is completely dry, add paint splatters to one area, using a smaller paintbrush. Water down the acrylic paint just a bit, and tap the end of the paintbrush over the area where you want the splatters. Let the paint dry completely.

STEP 5 Add motivational words. Print the words in your font of choice. Use a sharpened pencil to copy the letters directly onto the frame. I like to start with the last word of the phrase, which gives me a better idea of where to place the first word.

STEP 6 Trace the words with a black watercolor pencil, darkening them as much as possible. If varnishing, do so before removing the painter's tape. Your mirror is ready to use!

Pennant Banner

SUPPLIES
- White primed canvas triangles (approx. 6 ½" x 9" each)
- Paintbrushes
- Acrylic paint (various colors)
- Pencil and eraser
- Stencil patterns (various)
- White or black watercolor crayon
- Clothespins (small, medium, or regular size)
- Twine (any color)

STEP 1 If you're not using precut triangles, I suggest creating a cardboard template to trace triangles onto white primed canvas. Trace and cut out as many triangles as you would like for your banner.

ARTIST TIP
White primed canvas typically comes on a roll and can usually be purchased either by the roll or by the yard. Some art & craft stores also carry packs of precut canvas or fabric triangles, which would also work great for this project!

STEP 2 Be bold and bright! Use acrylic paint to paint vibrant colors on each pennant. It's okay to let some white show through in a few places. Let the background colors dry completely before moving to the next step.

STEP 3 Next go stencil crazy! Use contrasting colors to paint patterns on the pennants. I used two different stencils to complete mine. Allow the stenciled designs to dry completely. If you want to add more color to your pennants, you can go over some of them again with a third color—or add paint splatters!

ARTIST TIP

For the stenciled patterns, it works well to use colors that are a shade or two darker or lighter than the background colors. For instance, try orange on pink, light blue on green, etc.

STEP 4 If you're adding a word to your banner, use a pencil to draw a letter on each triangle. Then fill in the letters with acrylic paint, using a very small brush. Let the letters dry.

STEP 5 Roughly outline each letter with a sharpened watercolor crayon.

STEP 6 If you choose, varnish the artwork outside with adult supervision. When the varnish is dry, tie a looped knot, as shown, at the ends of the twine on each side of the pennant so it can hang on a wall.

STEP 7 Clip each pennant onto the twine with two clothespins. You can also use washi tape or decorative masking tape to attach your finished banner to the wall.

Paper Animal Painting

SUPPLIES

- 14" x 14" white canvas
- Acrylic paint (various colors)
- Paintbrushes
- Gesso
- Palette knife
- Watercolor paper or specialty handmade paper
- Scrapbook paper (optional)
- Pencil and eraser
- Mod Podge
- Small, fine-tipped plastic squeeze tube (optional)
- Black and white watercolor crayons
- Black oil pastel

STEP 1 Start by painting the background a bold, vibrant color! Let a little bit of white canvas show through in places; the "unfinished" background adds more texture. I used three different shades of blue, swirling them all together on the canvas with a large paintbrush.

STEP 2 Once the background is completely dry, use a paintbrush to add a strip of white gesso on the bottom. Let the gesso dry, and then brush on green paint for the grass.

ARTIST TIP
Cutting the paper to the same size as the canvas helps ensure the size of the animal is right when you're ready to draw. You can save excess paper for future projects!

STEP 3 Cut watercolor or other medium-weight paper to the same size as your canvas. If you're using specialty handmade paper that is already colored or has a pattern on it, you may not want to add any paint. If you're using watercolor paper like I did, paint it to "match" your animal. I used watered-down acrylic paint and watercolor paint in brown, cream, and various yellows.

STEP 4 Let the background dry before adding any other paint elements, such as cream splatters. I watered down cream acrylic paint and used a medium paintbrush to tap paint over the paper. Once the background is completely dry, draw your animal with a pencil.

STEP 5 Cut out the shape of the animal and glue it onto the canvas with Mod Podge, using a layer under the animal and on top. Press firmly and apply as many layers of Mod Podge as needed until all the edges are glued down. Then add some paper flowers or other designs.

STEP 6 Use a small, fine-tipped plastic squeeze tube filled with slightly watered down black acrylic paint to outline the flowers. (You can also use a black marker or watercolor crayon.) Outline the tiger with a sharpened watercolor crayon.

STEP 7 The finishing touches make a big difference! Add darker green to the grass for a "striped" look. Then roughly outline the stripes and the top of the grass with black oil pastel, smearing it in some places. Use the oil pastel to add stripes and a face to the tiger! Then use black and white watercolor crayons to draw stems and leaves for the flowers and outline the blossoms.

STEP 8 Add some final touches of color. Dip the handle end of a large paintbrush in orange acrylic paint and stamp on the flower centers. Then use a palette knife to add a few bursts of purple—or the color of your choice—to the edges of the canvas.

Inspirational Plaque

SUPPLIES

- Precut craft wood (approx. 3" x 7")
- Scrapbook paper or specialty handmade paper
- Printed words or magazine cutouts
- Scissors
- Acrylic paint (various colors)
- Mod Podge
- Paintbrush
- Black watercolor crayon
- Black oil pastel
- Small drill*
- 16-gauge crafting/jewelry wire
- Jewelry wire cutters
- Flat-nose jewelry pliers
- Various pieces of yarn and/or ribbon
- Beads (optional)

*Adult supervision required

STEP 1 Cut scrapbook or specialty paper to the same size as the wood. Then brush Mod Podge on the wood, place the paper on top, and press firmly to flatten. Add a coat or two of Mod Podge on top of the decorative paper as well. If needed, trim any excess paper off the edges.

STEP 2 Once the background paper is completely dry, use your fingers to rub acrylic paint on it. You only need a little paint; dip your fingers in water if you need to thin the paint. Once dry, add some paint splatters.

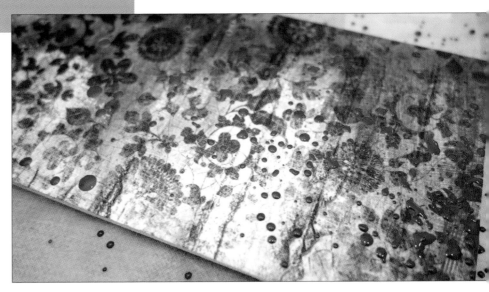

STEP 3 Once the paint is completely dry, cut out letters from a magazine or printout to create a word on your piece. Position the letters and adhere with Mod Podge, using a coat underneath and on top of each letter. Allow the letters to dry completely before roughly outlining the edges with a black watercolor crayon. This makes the letters stand out more against the patterned background.

STEP 4 Rub a black oil pastel along the edges of the wood and use your fingers to rub or smear the black, giving the edges a burnt look.

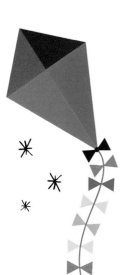

STEP 5 If varnishing, let dry before drilling a small hole in the top corner of each side.

STEP 6 Use 16-gauge crafting/jewelry wire and jewelry wire cutters to create a "handle" for the wood plaque. Tie small pieces of fabric, yarn, or ribbon all along the wire. You can also string beads onto the wire before closing the other end.

Art Wall Mobile

SUPPLIES

- 9 pieces of cardboard (4.25" x 5.25")
- Utility or craft knife*
- Gesso
- Pencil and sharpener
- Hole punch
- Paintbrushes
- Acrylic paint (various colors)
- Stencil patterns
- Small plastic squeeze tube (with fine tip)
- Black fine-tipped pigment ink pen or permanent marker
- Natural twine (twelve 6-inch strips and three 8-inch strips)
- Sturdy branch or wood stick (approximately 14" long)

*Adult supervision required

STEP 1 Make a 4.25" x 5.25" template out of regular paper and trace nine rectangles onto sturdy cardboard. Carefully cut them out with a utility or craft knife.

STEP 2 Lay the rectangles on your workspace in three rows of three, which is how the mobile will hang on the wall. Coat each rectangle with gesso, and allow it to dry completely.

ARTIST TIP
Keep your mobile laid out the way you will hang it on the wall when it is finished. This will help you keep your artwork in order!

STEP 3 Mark a dot for each hole punch, where the pieces will tie together. There should be no holes on the bottom of the last row or on the outer sides of the mobile.

STEP 4 Punch the holes out of the cardboard pieces. Now the fun begins! Paint a background color on each piece. Once they dry, add designs. You can splatter paint, use stencils as textured backgrounds, or add dripping paint. Try to make each rectangle different, and use coordinating colors.

STEP 5 Add some small images to your rectangles. I added just a few images on some of mine. For example, I added stars in the first rectangle, flowers in the third, and a heart with wings in the last. The rest of my rectangles will have only words, but you can add more images and designs if you choose!

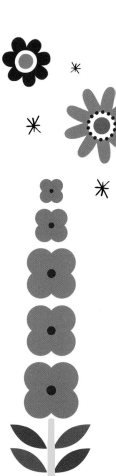

STEP 6 Next use a sharpened pencil to write words or phrases on the rectangles. You might use words from a poem, song lyrics, inspirational quotes, or a nursery rhyme. The sky is the limit! Get creative, and experiment with your lettering! Words can be in bubble type, cursive handwriting, or block type. You choose!

STEP 7 Next add color to the letters. You can use paint, permanent markers, or fine-tipped pigment ink pens to fill in or trace your letters. Once the letters are dry, feel free to add any extra details, such as a light border or more paint splatters.

STEP 8 When everything is completely dry, varnish. Then tie the rectangles together with twelve 6-inch pieces of twine. Use three 8-inch pieces of twine to tie the artwork onto the branch. Trim off any excess twine, and your new masterpiece is ready to hang.

ARTIST TIP

If you'd like more color, try using fabric strips to tie and hang your art instead of twine!

71

Picture Frame

SUPPLIES
- Blank wood frame
- Gesso
- Acrylic paint (various colors)
- Paintbrushes
- Decorative stencil (optional)
- Scrapbook paper
- Mod Podge
- Black watercolor pencil or watercolor crayon

STEP 1 Paint a layer of white gesso on the wood frame first. Once the gesso is dry, pick a vibrant color and paint the whole frame. Allow the paint to dry completely.

STEP 2 Use a decorative stencil to add a pattern to the frame. I used a lighter shade of purple acrylic paint to match the dark purple background. Let the paint dry.

STEP 3 Draw simple shapes, such as hearts and stars, on scrapbook paper that matches your frame. Then cut out the shapes and arrange them on the frame.

STEP 4 Use Mod Podge under and over the shapes to glue them to the frame. Once dry, add some paint splatters. Let the paint dry. Then outline the shapes and add any words with black or white watercolor pencil.

Magnetic Board

SUPPLIES

- Metal cookie sheet
- Map pages (from an atlas)
- Decorative tissue paper
- Printed words (from a home office printer)
- Mod Podge
- Black watercolor pencil or watercolor crayon
- Hot glue gun*
- D-ring hanger

* Adult supervision required

STEP 1 Begin by gluing a few map pages onto the cookie sheet. Use a large brush to apply a generous coat of Mod Podge directly on the cookie sheet. Press the map pages smooth on the sheet, and then add a coat of Mod Podge on top of the pages.

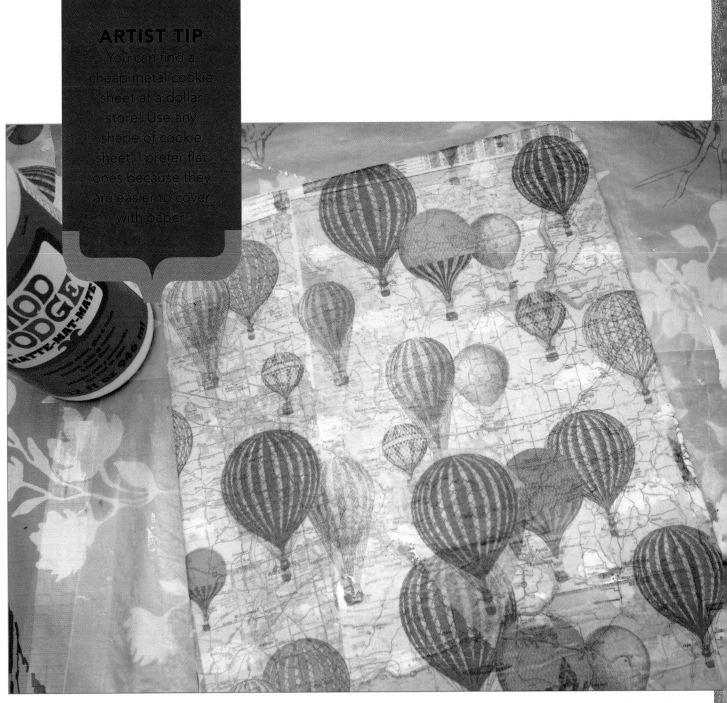

ARTIST TIP
You can find a cheap metal cookie sheet at a dollar store! Use any shape of cookie sheet. I prefer flat ones because they are easier to cover with paper.

STEP 2 While the Mod Podge is still wet, add decorative tissue paper on top of the map pages. Tissue paper tears easily, so work with it gently. Add another layer of Mod Podge on top of the tissue paper and let it dry completely. Then trim off any excess paper around the edges.

NOT ALL THOSE WHO WANDER ARE LOST

- J. R. R. Tolkien

STEP 3 Next add the words of your choice. You can use a home printer to write your own words, or you can cut out words from a magazine. Use Mod Podge under and on top of the words to attach them to the sheet. Let them dry, and then outline the words with a black watercolor crayon or pencil.

STEP 4 Attach a D-ring hanger to the back of the cookie sheet with a hot glue gun.

STEP 5 If varnishing your board, let it dry before hanging. Add a few magnets and use the board to post pictures, artwork, or anything else you want to display!

Watercolor Butterfly Tree

SUPPLIES

- 14" x 14" white canvas
- Pencil and eraser
- Paintbrushes
- Acrylic paint
- Rough watercolor paper
- Black fine-point permanent marker
- Watercolor paint
- Scissors
- Small hole punch
- Large heavy-duty needle* and heavy-duty thread

*Adult supervision required

STEP 1 Draw a tree on the canvas with your pencil.

STEP 2 Pick a bright color and paint the background with acrylic paint. Let some of the paint drip down one side of the canvas.

STEP 3 Next paint the tree, using a small paintbrush to stay inside the lines.

STEP 4 Draw about 26 butterflies on rough watercolor paper, using a fine-point permanent black marker. Make them all different sizes, shapes, and patterns!

STEP 5 Add color to the butterflies with watercolor paint or thinned acrylic paint. Let the paint dry completely.

STEP 6 Cut out the butterflies. They don't need to perfect; it's just fine to leave some of the white watercolor paper showing, especially around the antennae! Punch four holes in a zigzag pattern in the center of each butterfly.

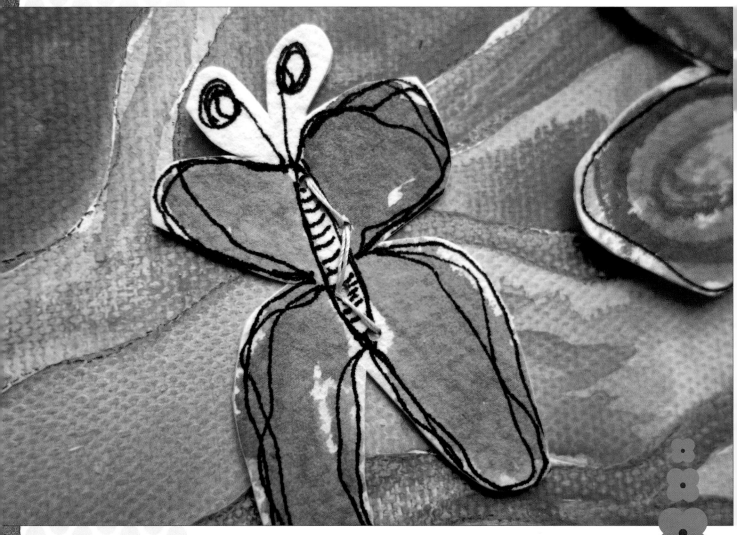

STEP 7 Use heavy-duty thread to stitch the butterflies onto the canvas in a random pattern.

STEP 8 If you'd like, use a watercolor pencil or crayon to add a short message or phrase to complete your artwork!

Guitar Painting

SUPPLIES

- 9" x 12" or 11" x 14" canvas
- Music-related images, scrapbook paper, and magazine images
- Mod Podge
- Pencil and eraser
- Acrylic paint (various colors)
- Black watercolor pencil
- White and black watercolor crayons
- Black oil pastel

ARTIST TIP

You can use images from just about anywhere in this mixed media painting! Find images on the Internet, in magazines, or make photocopies of your favorite CD covers. Simply get creative and be inspired by your favorite songs, bands, instruments, and musicians!

STEP 1 Cut or tear out images and papers, and arrange them on the canvas. Glue them in place with a layer of Mod Podge. Apply another layer of Mod Podge on top, pressing into place so the edges don't curl up. Let the canvas dry.

STEP 2 Use a pencil or watercolor pencil to draw the outline of a guitar. Keep it simple! My outline is kind of sketchy, and that's okay. You'll cover most of the sketch when you start adding color. Just be sure the outline is dark enough to see.

STEP 3 Use your finger to start adding color to the background. You can use a paintbrush too, but I like to use my finger because it gives me more control. Don't completely cover the background images with paint—just a thin coat will do!

STEP 4 When the background is done, do the same with the guitar. I didn't put any paint in the center of my guitar so the natural color of the images shows through.

STEP 5 Let the paint dry. Then outline the guitar with a black oil pastel. Smear the pastel by rubbing your finger along the outline. This softens the outline so it doesn't look too perfect or bold.

STEP 6 For the final touches, add paint splatters in random places on the edges. Then add a squiggly white outline around the guitar with a white watercolor crayon.

Glass Art Planter

SUPPLIES

- Small glass votive
  (approx. 4" x 4" x 4" or larger)
- Scrapbook or specialty handmade paper
- Scissors
- Mod Podge
- Paintbrush
- Black acrylic paint
- Printed words or magazine cutouts
- Black watercolor pencil or crayon

STEP 1 Cut the paper that you want to use as close to size as you can. I selected three different papers. Work on one side at a time to apply the paper with Mod Podge.

STEP 2 Adhere a piece of paper to each side. Don't forget to use Mod Podge both underneath and on top of the paper!

ARTIST TIP
Work with a sheet of wax paper under your planter so that the glass doesn't stick to your work surface during the gluing process.

STEP 3 Once the paper is completely dry, splatter black paint on the side where you plan to put your words. This is optional—I like to add paint splatters to everything! Remember to water down the paint so that it splatters easily off the brush.

STEP 4 After the paint dries, add words. You can use words cut from a magazine or print words on a home printer. Glue them onto the planter with Mod Podge, applying a coat both underneath and on top of the paper.

STEP 5 Once dry, roughly outline the words with a sharpened black watercolor crayon or watercolor pencil.

STEP 6 If you choose to varnish your planter, be sure to do so before filling it with the plant of your choice!

Field of Flowers

SUPPLIES

- 11" x 14" white canvas
- Paintbrushes
- Acrylic paint (various colors)
- Pencil and eraser
- Scrapbook or specialty handmade paper
- Printed words or magazine cutouts
- Scissors
- Mod Podge
- Black watercolor crayon
- Black oil pastel

STEP 1 Start by adding drips of watered-down paint all over the top of the canvas. These drips will act as flower stems! Dip your fingers into a cup of water and then the paint, and flick splatters of paint onto the canvas. Work from bottom to top, so that the splatters look as though they are moving upward. Let the paint dry completely.

STEP 2 Turn the canvas so that the band of green is at the bottom. Cut out paper circles and ovals for flowers. Cut out a butterfly, bird, or other insect and animal shapes. I drew my bird on scrapbook paper and found the butterfly image on another piece of paper. Cut out letters from a magazine (or print them from a home printer) to create a word or phrase. Lay everything on the canvas first to make sure you're happy with the layout.

STEP 3 Glue all the paper images to the canvas with Mod Podge, applying a coat underneath and on top of each piece. Make sure all of the edges are pressed down. Once dry, use a small paintbrush to add contrasting color to the grass area. I watered down blue paint to make it more like watercolor paint. I also added extra splatters of paint near the bird.

ARTIST TIP

Don't forget to use your imagination! You can use my example as a starting point, but make the piece your own by choosing your favorite colors.

STEP 4 Once all of the paint is dry, roughly outline the flower circles with black oil pastel, and gently smear the pastel all around the circles. Use a black watercolor crayon to roughly outline the bird, flower stems, letters, and butterfly.

Flowerpot Magnets

SUPPLIES

- Tile pieces
- Acrylic paint (various colors)
- Paintbrushes
- Black watercolor crayon
- Fabric scraps
- Small felt sheet
- Decorative paper
- Mod Podge
- Decorative stencil (optional)
- 16-gauge jewelry wire
- Jewelry wire cutters*
- Round magnet for ceramic use
- Hot glue gun*

*Adult supervision required

ARTIST TIP

These tile pieces come on a netted sheet and are considered border tile for kitchens and bathrooms. You can find them at home improvement stores.

STEP 1 There are lots of tile shapes to choose from—pick the ones that you like the most. Then make your mark! You can splatter paint, paint with a brush, or simply rub on some paint with your fingers. I added a second color to one of my pieces by using a stencil and a paintbrush.

STEP 2 Cut out circles from fabric scraps and assemble the flowers. Start with a fabric back, and then use paper or a second layer of fabric for the inner circle. Glue the layers together with Mod Podge, working on a sheet of wax paper to protect your work surface. Add a final layer of Mod Podge on top of the finished flowers. Getting glue on the backside of the fabric flower will also help stiffen the petals a little.

STEP 3 Once the flowers are completely dry, add the centers. Use acrylic paint to make a large dot in the center of each flower. You can even add smaller dots around the flowers or a thin layer of paint if you choose! Allow the paint to dry before moving on.

STEP 4 Cut out a felt back for each flower that matches its size. You can also use the felt backing as another flower layer and make it a little bit bigger if you wish. Cut jewelry wire into pieces that are 3" to 3½" long. Place the wire stem between the fabric flower and the felt back and hot glue all three of them together. Now the flower looks like a lollipop! Complete this step for each flower.

STEP 5 For this project, I recommend you varnish the flowerpots (not the flowers). When the flowerpots are completely dry, hot glue the flower stems and magnets to the backs of the tile pieces. The stems should be sandwiched between the tile piece and the magnet.

ARTIST TIP
The colors on your "flowerpots" will evolve as you pick out fabric and paper for the flowers. Throughout this project, I found myself rubbing more color on the blue flowerpot, and I decided to add the word "Love" to the orange and pink flowerpot with a black watercolor crayon.

STEP 6 Once the hot glue dries, your magnets are ready to use on the refrigerator or other magnetic surface! You can use these magnets to post your favorite artwork or photographs.

Artful Craft Caddy

SUPPLIES
- Cardboard bottle carrier
- Gesso
- Paintbrushes
- Acrylic paint (various colors)
- Pencil and eraser
- Stencil
- Black watercolor crayon or oil pastel

STEP 1 For this artful craft caddy, you can use any type of cardboard drink carrier from the grocery store. Start by painting a thin coat of white gesso all over the outside of the carrier. You can paint the inside as well if you like, but it will soon be filled with fun, artsy stuff!

STEP 2 Once the gesso is dry, paint the background colors. I chose bright, cheery yellow and green so that other colors will "pop" against them. You can use any colors you wish.

STEP 3 When the paint is dry, start adding design details. Use a pencil to trace a stencil or draw your own designs onto the caddy. You don't have to copy the stencil exactly as it is—pick and choose which parts you like.

STEP 4 Use a small paintbrush to paint the design with bright, bold colors. Paint around the caddy with one color at a time. Let the paint dry completely.

STEP 5 Roughly outline the shapes with a black watercolor crayon or oil pastel.

STEP 6 If varnishing
your caddy, let dry
before stocking with
all your favorite art
supplies!

Chunky Word Canvas

SUPPLIES

- 8" x 10" white canvas panel
- Acrylic paint (various colors)
- Gesso
- Paintbrushes
- Palette knife
- Glass bead gel
- Molding paste
- Pencil and eraser
- Black watercolor crayon or pencil
- Black fine-tipped and medium-tipped pigment ink markers
- 8" x 10" picture frame (optional)

STEP 1 Lightly brush several shades of blue paint on the blank canvas with a paintbrush. Then add contrast by rubbing in additional shades of blue paint with a paper towel. Leave a little bit of white to add dimension and texture!

STEP 2 Draw a few clouds on the canvas with a pencil. Then fill them in with white paint. Let the paint dry, and erase any pencil marks.

STEP 3 Mix molding paste with a few shades of yellow paint, using the palette knife.
Scoop paint on the knife and add a chunky sun. Then add a few strokes of orange paint.

105

STEP 4 Draw a bird on the canvas. Keep the shape simple, with an oval for the bottom and a circle for the head. Don't forget the beak and tail! Paint the bird with gesso or white paint.

STEP 5 Once dry, paint the bird any color you wish! I used several shades of red and pink, blending the colors together as I painted. Mix molding paste with two shades of green and use a palette knife to add strokes of grass.

STEP 6 Now incorporate glass bead gel into your artwork for some extra sparkle and texture! I brushed the gel onto the sun and the bird's wing. Once the gel dries completely, you can add more color on top of it.

STEP 7 Once dry, use a pencil to add words from a phrase, poem, or song. Try making each word look different!

STEP 8 Use fine-tipped and medium-tipped black pigment ink markers to outline and fill in the words.

you are my sunshine my only sunshine

STEP 9 To finish, outline the bird with a sharpened watercolor crayon or pencil. Then add a hint of color around the edges. I mixed glass bead gel with purple paint and used a palette knife to add splashes of color.

Birds on a Wire

SUPPLIES

- 16" x 16" white canvas
- Paintbrushes
- Acrylic paint (various colors)
- Spray bottle with water
- Paper towel
- Pencil and eraser
- Yardstick (or ruler longer than 12")
- Small plastic squeeze tube (with fine tip)
- Scrapbook or specialty handmade paper
- Mod Podge
- Black watercolor crayon
- Stencil or decorative stamp (optional)
- Dictionary page (optional)

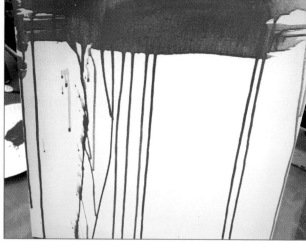

STEP 1 Go ahead and make your mark with a splash of vibrant color across the top of a 16" x 16" canvas. I chose yellow because it is light enough for other colors to be added on top. Use a large brush to swipe watered-down yellow across the top of the canvas, holding the canvas upright so the paint starts to drip. Using a spray bottle, spray water on the canvas to encourage the paint to drip even more. Keep going until you're happy with the background. Let the paint dry completely.

STEP 2 Add a second vibrant color. I chose red—the bolder, the better! Use a large paintbrush to swipe your second color across the canvas, letting it drip down and mix with the first color. Keep a good amount of water on your brush to help the paint drip. While the paint is wet, add some splatters in random places throughout the canvas. Remember that the paint must be watered down in order for the color to splatter off the brush.

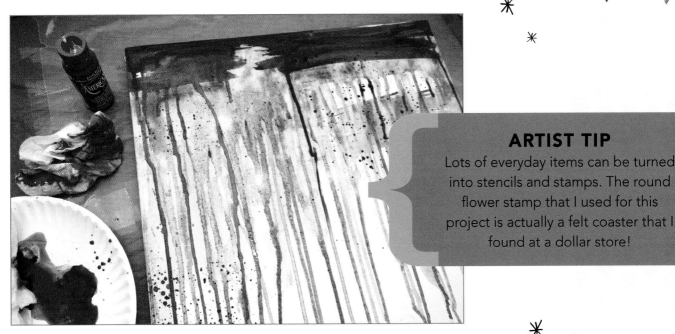

ARTIST TIP
Lots of everyday items can be turned into stencils and stamps. The round flower stamp that I used for this project is actually a felt coaster that I found at a dollar store!

STEP 3 After the second layer of color is completely dry, add a third color. I used hot pink this time. Paint a layer of the new color on top of the red and use the spray bottle to make it spread all over the canvas. Then use a paper towel to blot the paint in random places. Let the painting dry completely.

STEP 4 Use a stencil or rubber stamp to add texture to the painting. Apply a coat of paint directly onto the stamp with a brush, and then stamp the canvas in random places. I stamped with the same red color that I used for my second layer of paint. Don't water down the paint for the stamping; the image should come up bold against the vibrant background. Let the painting dry completely.

STEP 5 Once dry, add the wire and the birds. Use a sharpened pencil and a yardstick to draw lines for the two wires. Then draw the birds. You can draw the birds freehand, or you can create and trace cutouts. To create the cutouts, I found bird silhouette images on the Internet, printed them, and cut them out to use as templates.

STEP 6 Next glue strips of dictionary pages (or other paper) to the bottom of the canvas, using Mod Podge both under and on top of the paper. Instead of cutting the paper, I chose to rip the top edges of the sheets to create a rough edge.

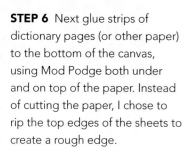

STEP 7 While the paper strips dry, fill in the birds with black paint. Use a very small paintbrush and try to stay inside the lines. For the wires, try using a small plastic squeeze tube with a fine tip instead of a paintbrush.

STEP 8 When the Mod Podge is dry, paint some fun flowers at the bottom of the canvas. I painted some simple black stems and circles with turquoise paint for the centers. Add more splatters near the flowers, using the same color. You can also use decorative paper circles in the centers of your flowers instead. Once dry, use a black watercolor crayon to add squiggles to the rough edges of the paper strip.

▶ **STEP 9** Once complete, sign your masterpiece!

114

Hand-painted Greeting Card

SUPPLIES
- Canvas fabric (two squares)
- Patterned fabric (two squares)
- Pencil and eraser
- Acrylic or watercolor paints (various colors)
- Paintbrushes
- Small fine-tipped squeeze tube
- Fabric glue
- Watercolor paper or other heavyweight paper
- Black marker
- 3 decorative brads
- Grommet or eyelet pliers

STEP 1 Paint one side of the two canvas squares, using the colors of your choosing. Try mixing two or three colors from a similar color family. Add drops and splatters if you wish. My squares are 7.5" x 7.5"—you can make your card as big or as small as you want!

STEP 2 Let the paint dry completely. If the edges curled up, you may need an adult to help you iron the squares smooth again. Then add your design. I chose a heart! Draw your design in pencil. Then fill it in with white paint to create a nice background for other paint colors.

STEP 3 Let the white paint dry, and then paint your design with any color you choose. The white paint helps my blue heart appear more vibrant on the already-vibrant background.

STEP 4 Next add your special message. You can write it in pencil first, and then follow the pencil lines with a fine-tipped squeeze tube filled with acrylic paint and a tiny bit of water. I also added a decorative heart and scroll to the back of my card.

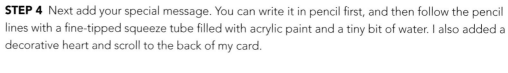

STEP 5 Once the art is completely dry, glue pieces of patterned fabric to the back sides of the canvas squares. Cut the fabric to the same size as the canvas, and glue it to the back of the canvas with fabric glue. While the fabric glue dries, work on the message for the inside of your card. I like to use watercolor paper for the inside because it adds extra texture. You can trace your message with a black marker if you wish.

STEP 6 Once your fabric glue is completely dry, mark holes for the brads, which will hold the greeting card together. Eyelet/grommet pliers are perfect for punching holes in thicker fabrics—these pliers make it easy! Once the holes are punched, slip the brads in place.

STEP 7 Now your hand-painted card is ready to share with someone special! You can make these fun cards for any occasion—birthdays, teacher gifts, Grandparent's Day. You can even make a mini book of poetry!

I HOPE YOU HAVE A WONDERFUL BIRTHDAY

Follow Your Heart

SUPPLIES

- Precut craft wood
  (approx. 4.25" x 4.25")
- Paintbrush
- Acrylic paint (various colors)
- Scrapbook paper or
  specialty handmade paper
- Decorative ribbon or washi tape
- Heavy watercolor paper
- Printed words or magazine cutouts
- Scissors
- Mod Podge
- Black watercolor pencil or crayon
- Small drill*
- 16-gauge crafting/jewelry wire
- Jewelry wire cutters
- Flat-nose jewelry pliers
- Hot glue gun*
- Small trinkets/embellishments
- Various pieces of yarn and/or ribbon
  (optional)
- Beads (optional)
- Gel medium, matte (optional)

*Adult supervision required

STEP 1 Start by adding a quick coat of paint to the front of the square. I used blue and experimented by adding texture to the background with dark brown paint and a decorative stencil. After about a minute, I rubbed off the brown paint with a paper towel, leaving just a hint of pattern on the blue.

STEP 2 Once the paint is completely dry, add a few strips of torn paper with Mod Podge. I also added a strip of zigzag washi tape. While the paper/tape is drying, create some splatters on a piece of heavy watercolor paper to use for a heart cutout.

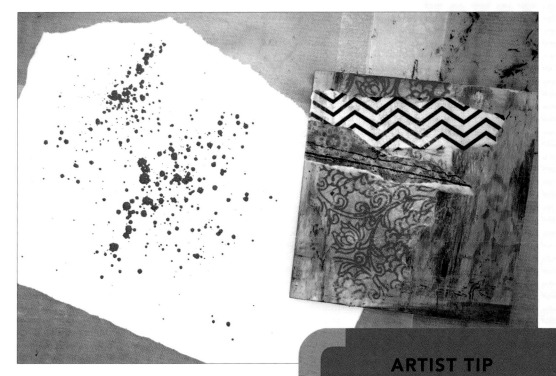

ARTIST TIP

Treat washi tape like you would a piece of paper. While it isn't necessary to use Mod Podge under the washi tape, be sure to apply a coat or two on top so it stays in place.

STEP 3 Once the splatters are completely dry, cut out a heart shape and use Mod Podge under and over it to glue it onto the wood. Then add printed words to your art. I used word strips printed on regular printer paper, but you can also use words cut out from a magazine!

Ideas for Embellishments

- Decorative key
- Painted mini domino
- Small painted/decorated wooden shapes
- Anything from the scrapbook section of an art & craft store that is small enough to fit on the art!

STEP 4 When everything is dry, roughly outline the words with a sharpened black watercolor pencil or crayon. If varnishing, let the varnish dry before drilling two small holes in the top corners. Use 16-gauge crafting/jewelry wire and jewelry pliers to create a "handle" for your wood art. If you want to add beads, string them onto the other end before closing the handle.

STEP 5 Add any last-minute embellishments. I added two mini hearts, using a hot glue gun. I also added a strip of decorative ribbon at the bottom, using gel medium. A combination of yarn, ribbon, and fabric tied off to one side adds an eclectic touch to the finished piece of art.

Repurposed Canvas Bookmarks

Canvas art bookmarks make great gifts for teachers, friends, and grandparents! If you start a canvas and don't like the way it is turning out—or simply want to repurpose old art—cut up the canvas and make bookmarks! All you need is some extra fabric and some small embellishments to bring these creative gifts to life!

SUPPLIES
- Unused/unwanted canvas
- Fabric scraps
- Scissors
- Ribbon, twine, or yarn
- Grommet/eyelet punch
- Fabric adhesive
- Sewing machine* (optional)

*Adult supervision required

▶ Remove the entire canvas you wish to repurpose from its wooden frame. For each bookmark, cut a 7.5" x 2" rectangle. Cut fabric to the same size as the bookmark and either sew the two strips together or glue them together with fabric adhesive. Let the fabric adhesive dry before punching a hole at the top of the bookmark with an eyelet punch or heavy-duty hole punch. Then add yarn, twine, or ribbon to complete!

Embellishing the Bookmarks

▶ Using a sewing machine to stitch the fabric and canvas together creates a nice finished edge, but fabric adhesive also works well!

▶ Cut shapes out of the canvas and sew, hot glue, or hand stitch them onto other art projects for a one-of-a-kind finishing touch!

▲ Add finishing touches to the bookmark by adding words (printed on paper and attached with Mod Podge) or drawing on it with paint or a watercolor crayon!

ARTIST TIP
You can also use repurposed canvas to create gift tags!

The End

Now that you've reached the end of this book, what will you create next? Mixed media art is all about experimenting, imagining, and creating with passion! You have the freedom to create as you wish and to explore as you choose, and you will learn so much along the way. Unleash the explorer in you. Be bold. Be brave. Be fearless. Live artfully!